Inspirations
from a Paper Boat

Conversations with a Loving Father

Virginia Duhanes

Inspirations from a Paper Boat

Published by
The Leprosy Mission International
80 Windmill Road, Brentford
Middlesex TW8 0QH, United Kingdom

Edited and distributed by TLM Trading Limited
(see inside back cover for details).

First Published 2007, reprinted 2007
© Virginia Duhanes, text and photos

Virginia Duhanes has asserted her right to be identified
as the author of this work in accordance with the Copyright,
Designs and Patents Act, 1988

All rights and subsidiary rights have been granted to
The Leprosy Mission International

Bible quotations are from the NEW INTERNATIONAL VERSION,
by permission of the International Bible Society.

Editorial and Design by Creative Plus Publishing Ltd,
2nd Floor, 151 High Street, Billericay, Essex, CM12 9AB
www.creative-plus.co.uk

Printed and bound in China
Phoenix Offset

A catalogue record for this book is available from the British Library.
ISBN 0 902731 65 3

Foreword

I first sat down to read *Inspirations from a Paper Boat* rather as one would approach a novel. The emotions that hit me were totally unexpected and profound. Here was a collection of written illustrations and images given voice from our heavenly Father. Each one was so relevant, so loving and spoke directly to my spirit. I loved the pictures, but I loved more the voice of God. It comes through each page as a constant reminder that he is faithful and unchanging. There is nothing in this book that isn't in line with my understanding of Scripture and throughout you perceive that the visual, the voice and the word of God are being knitted together to bring us a new understanding.

Virginia's writing is extremely descriptive and you feel you are 'there', experiencing the events as they happen. She has tested, tried and measured these stories against Scripture and has been prayerful in her response to God's voice. I cannot recommend this book more highly. You'll find many of the images stay in the front of your mind and will encourage you throughout the day.

This book inspired me to make a fresh attempt at listening to God through 'picture images' and echo the words given by the Lord to Virginia, *'I gave you your imagination as a gift. It is the pond over which I push my paper boats to you!'*

Julie Sheldon, Author of *Dancer Off Her Feet* (Hodder and Stoughton)

This is one of the most unusual and delightful little books I have yet had the pleasure of reading. It is full of colour, charm and interest but it can also be taken in short bites which makes it an ideal bedside companion.

On each page, Virginia takes you by the hand, letting you see the world through her eyes. Then, very gently and unobtrusively, she leads you right back to the very heart of all the beauty you have just seen, right to the Creator Himself. I loved this book and want to read it many times over in the years to come.

Jennifer Rees Larcombe, Author of *Unexpected Healing* (Hodder and Stoughton)

Introduction

It was whilst I was on an Alpha course at Holy Trinity Church, Brompton, London in February 1984 that I first learnt about God's Holy Spirit and I invited Him to come and dwell in my heart. He came – and soon I began to hear His gentle inward voice; through reading the Bible which had come alive to me and through 'images' that He dropped into my mind. I learned to tune my ear to recognise His voice and to trust the different ways He began to communicate with me.

Occasionally, He'd speak so clearly it would be like having a conversation with a friend; at other times, He'd prompt me to go to a certain place and, once there, He would speak through something He'd point out to me. Many of the following thoughts were written whilst on holiday in France – in special times of silence and solitude that for me were so essential to being able to hear Him: others were inspired by letters I'd written to God and by what I believe was His response to them. I realised how much the Lord wanted an intimate relationship with me, and how precious His words were – so I kept journals of everything He said – for me there is nothing more exciting than hearing the voice of God.

However, in these early days of 'hearing His voice' and receiving 'picture images' I was very concerned that my vivid imagination did not deceive me – that everything I believed I had heard would be the truth and would only reflect the integrity of the Bible. So, I asked the Lord one day, *"Is my imagination a good thing or is it a dangerous thing that will lead me astray?"* His reply seemed crystal clear to me...
"I gave you your imagination as a gift.
It is the pond over which I push My paper boats to you!"

Virginia Duhanes, February 2007

Dedication

For my special friend Caroline Weller, with all my love.

Contents

It is easy to hear my knocking on the door. I want you to hear the whispers from the hem of my robe, as I stand outside.

On a beautiful, sunny, spring morning in the Cotswolds, the cool dew-scented air was drenched in birdsong that echoed from deep within the mossy woods. Sue was leaving for the Palm Sunday service with her husband Andrew, the vicar, but just as she was about to get into the car, dressed in her best long tartan skirt, she had a feeling that she should go back and check the well-being of a pregnant ewe in their field. She discovered that one of them had gone into labour and crouching nearby, waiting, was a fox! For the next two hours, she and the fox sat on the dew-soaked grass together, watching patiently for the moment of birth.

As the parishioners came out of church they were met by a very cold, wet and dishevelled Sue, holding the new-born lamb tenderly in her long damp skirt, the ewe following closely behind her. I felt that God was giving me a picture message.

"I often speak to you by gently impressing your heart with my thoughts, but you sometimes ignore them, brushing them away as your own foolish ideas! But I need you to be sensitive to this new way of listening and obeying. Someone's life may depend on you being there at the right time for them.

I need you to be soft like a wet clay pot waiting to be embossed with the potter's character. Be soft, be still and be silent for this will help you to hear my thoughts. As a feather on the back of your hand, my messages sometimes come to you, almost imperceptibly. Don't respond with logic and reasoning for that will 'pluck the feathers off the bird' and my message will fall silently to the ground. Practise solitude, don't just listen to the birdsong that I know you love, but listen to the very stillness around you. Stillness is the foundation of all our music to you, silence the first requisite before any note can be played or heard.

My enemy prowls around seeking to destroy, discourage and to kill the very life I am bringing to birth through my children's lives. When you are sensitive to my voice you can stand between the 'fox and the lamb' with a prayer, telephone call or a written word of encouragement. I may ask you to drop what you're doing immediately, and go where I send you. It is easy to hear my knocking on the door. I want you to hear the whispers from the hem of my robe, as I stand outside."

Isaiah 55:3 Pay attention, come close now, listen carefully to my life-giving, life-nourishing words. I'm making a lasting covenant commitment with you, the same that I made with David: sure, solid, enduring love. (The Message)

Matthew 25:40 …I tell you the truth, whatever you did for the least of these brothers of mine, you did for me.

You can best know me as your Father, when you are willing to be like a child!

In the bright crisp early morning sunshine, the oranges glowed like fairy lights on the trees. I was heading towards a telephone box in the town square hoping to catch my husband in London before he started work. The dividing glass partition between my telephone box and the adjacent one had vanished and a young mother and child entered next to me.

The little French girl was wearing a bright red anorak, her face softly framed by its white lamb's wool trimming. Strands of silky blond hair escaped from under the hood, tickling her rosy cheeks, the faded pink drawstring cord was firmly grasped by her glistening, white teeth. She moved into 'my half' of the telephone box, blissfully unaware that there was meant to be a glass barrier between us; purity and innocence shone out of her crystal grey eyes as she looked up at me and smiled. She took the rather cold hand that I held out to her into her own warm, cushion-soft one, and held it with complete trust and love. In that moment, I didn't ever want her to let it go! When I left the phone box and walked away from her, we waved and blew kisses to each other until the orange trees finally hid her searching little face from my sight. God encouraged me through that small event.

"You only perceive a barrier between us when you think like an adult instead of being like this little child. How often you worry that you have displeased me in some way, or failed to come up to what you think are my expectations of you! You look at me with such fear in your eyes, and dare not come close to touch my outstretched hand.

I have destroyed this barrier between us once and forever by the shedding of my blood! I have set you free from guilt, fear and rejection and I so long for you to truly trust me. Not just to come over to 'my side' when you feel good about yourself but to stay close by me whatever your feelings may be! I love to see your shining, happy eyes seeking my face in such a trusting

way, you cannot imagine how much joy you give me. It hurts me when you sometimes become 'grown-up' and lose that spontaneous smile that welcomes me into your heart! Do you not realise, that having paid the greatest price for you, I will never ever allow a barrier to be put up again between us! Nothing that you do will ever stop me loving you.
I will never ever walk out on you, or let you out of my sight – no, not even for one moment!

Dare to cross over the barrier in your heart and take me at my word."

Mark 10:15 ...anyone who will not receive the kingdom of God like a little child will never enter it.

Romans 8:15 For you did not receive a spirit that makes you a slave again to fear, but you received the Spirit of sonship. And by him we cry, "Abba, Father."

Rest under my loving hand and I will show you the things that need to be cleared out of your life.

In my heart I laughed at the man with his metal detector. It was such a glorious morning on the beach – everything washed and sparkling, breathtakingly beautiful. The soft contours of the newly-raked sand had been disturbed by his footprints and the pigeons were scrambling in and out of the furrows with a lurching gait.

"Have you found anything," I called to him as I headed towards the sea for my early morning swim. "Deux centimes, Madame!" he replied with regret and a small Gallic shrug.

I pitied him wasting his time looking for treasure in such an unfruitful place, but as I swam out away from the shore, I felt that I was being rather critical. What did I know about his life or his needs, his daily search for something of value? In my heart, I felt God challenging me to think again.

"My Spirit is like that man on the beach, searching early each morning, for the hard, metallic pieces of 'shrapnel' in your heart. Not just the critical and selfish attitudes you sometimes have, but also the words that have wounded you – that have never been brought to the surface to be removed. These imprisoned barbs have done damage, not only to you, but through your habit of burying them alive, they have also, at the end of the day, damaged others.

As the high tide washes up the rubbish onto the beach, allowing it to be cleared away, so too my Spirit will bring to light those things that no longer belong in your walk with me. Deal with them when I reveal them, ask me to take them away and bring the healing power of my love to cleanse your heart. If you ignore them they will be drawn back once more into your subconscious, just as the high tide will gather up any debris that is left on the beach, taking it out again into deep waters.

Dare to feel the pain of these little stones in your heart, just as you feel the sharpness of a small pebble in your shoe. Rest under my loving hand and I will show you the things that need to be cleared out of your life. Don't look down on this poor man, rather ask me to reveal the treasure that he really is searching for – Myself."

Psalm 139:1 O LORD, you have searched me and you know me.

John 16:13 But when he, the Spirit of truth, comes, he will guide you into all truth.

Sometimes you will not be able to see my footprints - I may be walking on water!

Except for the pigeons darting back and forth over the soft sand, pecking amongst the entangled pieces of driftwood and rubbish, nothing moved on the beach. I was wrapped up warmly against gusts of chill air blowing off the snow-capped mountains of the French Alps, absorbing the peace and beauty of the sea and sky. The sound of the little icy waves tripping over each other on the shore was soothing. The icy, snow-starched peaks were brilliant white against a gentian sky; the sun warmed my upturned face.

I'd finished my picnic lunch, throwing the sweet juicy core of my pear towards the pigeons – which they ignored! Continuing their random pecking amongst plastic bottle caps and matted seaweed, I watched them as they made impulsive dashes towards the water's edge – like children chasing pigeons in the park! Rushing towards the waves over the damp smooth sand, I noticed with surprise that their pink scratchy feet left no mark at all and I sensed that God was drawing my attention to something special.

"Sometimes you will not be able to see my footprints – I may be walking on water! Look for me in the unexpected place. Don't despair or be discouraged when I don't appear to be acting on your behalf or answering your prayers. I have heard you. I know your thoughts even before you pray and they are precious to me.

I watched you pick up that piece of smooth green glass from its gritty setting of cold sand. You washed it in a ripple and held it up to the light, gazing through its emerald lens into the sky. You smiled. I too hold your thoughts, like the sparkling wet stones in your hand, that you sift with a

cold salty finger, pocketing the most precious to take home. Some give a moment's pleasure as they bounce over the glassy water, whilst the rest you let fall from your hand. But I gently hold all your prayers and thoughts, even the foolish ones, in my heart before I answer you.

Trust me to choose what is best for you. Let me take from your hand anything that will be of no value to you, that will burden you with more than you will need to carry home."

Job 13:27 ...you keep close watch on all my paths by putting marks on the soles of my feet.

Psalm 66:19 ...but God has surely listened and heard my voice in prayer.

This love that you desire to have for others is distilled through tears; the impatient and proud will never wait for it.

I have prayed for some people over many years, without seeing any visible change in their problems or sickness, and I've often been very tempted to give up. It is hard to persevere, year after year in prayer, when sometimes there is so little visible encouragement. On one occasion, whilst not seeing the results of my prayers for a married couple whom I love very much, I asked the Lord to show me why my prayers were not being answered.

In my mind, He showed me an image of an unfinished jigsaw puzzle on a table, with the lid beside it, showing the finished picture. It was of an idyllic English village scene. There was a river running through a meadow in the background, bordered by willow trees, in the foreground a village green with a duck pond in the middle, and behind, a row of thatched houses, each with its small flower-filled garden neatly enclosed by a white picket fence. In the centre of the picture was the village church, the cross on top of its steeple, plainly outlined against a

clear blue summer's sky. Looking down at my hand, 'I saw' that I was holding the piece of puzzle that had this 'cross' upon it, but I realised that it couldn't be 'put it into the picture' because there was, as yet, nothing to support it. Only the border had been joined together, creating an empty frame – waiting to be filled.

"My dear child, I know about your frustration at not seeing your prayers answered, but I know these loved ones for whom you are praying so much better than you do! I know and see every circumstance in their lives, both past, present and future. I know the order in which I am going to build up their trust in me, the ways in which I plan to do this, and how I will lead them into a place where they'll be able to open up their hearts to me.

There are many obstacles in the way, fears to be removed and barriers to be lifted in their minds. Many have such a distorted view of who I am, that they don't want to come close enough to let me love them. Whilst you keep faithfully praying for them, I will faithfully keep 'adding the pieces into the puzzle'. At the right moment, and not before, I will place my 'cross' into their lives and write my name upon their hearts.

Think of me as if I was going to meet them on the other side of a lake, and that your prayers are the hidden propeller under my boat! When you stop praying, the boat stops moving! So, don't ever give up, for I need your prayers to help me add the 'pieces into the puzzle'. You may only see the 'plain wooden underside' of their everyday lives, but I can see the finished picture from the lid of the box slowly developing."

Isaiah 30:15 ...in quietness and trust is your strength...

Luke 18:1 Then Jesus told his disciples a parable to show them that they should always pray and not give up.

I have given you a beautiful new wardrobe of clothes, yet you go back to wearing the old, familiar, comfortable garments of the past!

On a warm summer's afternoon in Notting Hill Gate, London, I was sitting in my car at the traffic lights. Walking towards me on the pavement came a young girl in a pair of very 'distressed' jeans – her thin white knees visible through the twinned fraying slashes, her whole attire seeming to shout "this is about as dirty, torn and dishevelled as I can look". Silver rings pierced her face and I thought to myself – or maybe I spoke aloud – "why on earth does she choose to look like that?" I was shocked to hear a still, gentle voice speak into my heart.

"You look like that sometimes."
"I don't ever look like that!" I replied.
"Yes you do," the quiet voice gently insisted.
"When have I ever looked like that?"

"When you go back to your old ways of thinking about yourself, as if you were a failure and second best. When you listen to the 'drum roll of fear' instead of my 'heartbeat of love' for you. When you think that you're bound to fail me, that you won't succeed in anything you do, or that I'll ask you to do the impossible – when did I ever ask you to 'leap through a flaming hoop'?

These ways of thinking 'clothe you in rags again'. I have given you a beautiful new wardrobe of clothes, yet you go back to wearing the old, familiar, comfortable garments of the past! Refuse to entertain the negative nasty thoughts you have and thank me that I am building your life up and not tearing you down. Dwell deeply on my love for you; this will help you get free from the fear that so often robs you of my peace and joy. Your life will not suddenly 'collapse like a house of cards', nor will your healing be taken away from you. Why would I take away what I gave you in love? I don't lend my gifts – I give them for you to enjoy and use.

You are not the daughter who made a mess of her life and received a poor measure but my daughter on whom the fullness of my blessing rests. You are not the daughter that was always ill but the child I always longed to heal. You are not like your father in his weaknesses for I have undone all the weak, negative, less-than-perfect things in your life. You are not average in height, ability, looks or size! This word average is not to exist any longer in your life. YOU are my perfect, my best – MY CHILD. I love you, my daughter – you resemble me."

Isaiah 61:10 I delight greatly in the LORD; my soul rejoices in my God. For he has clothed me with garments of salvation and arrayed me in a robe of righteousness, as a bridegroom adorns his head like a priest, and as a bride adorns herself with her jewels.

Philippians 1:6 ...he who began a good work in you will carry it on to completion until the day of Christ Jesus.

If you'll take the risk and leave the quiet waters of the harbour, I'll chart the course for you on the open sea.

It was deliciously cool early in the morning and no one was about. As I headed towards the harbour along the ancient walls of the stone ramparts, the screaming seagulls circled above the cathedral's tower that jutted out like a bastion high above the old French town of Antibes. I could hear the high-pitched pinging of the halyards against the ships' masts as the harbour came into view. The gulls swooped over the deep blue waters, the rising sun blushing their wings.

"Virginia, describe to me what you see."

"I see boats, all tied up at their moorings. They look in good repair, at least above the waterline. They're very close to each other, and each boat is facing in the right direction so as to be able to leave the harbour and go out to the open sea."

"Well, what do you think they are waiting for?"

"I imagine they're waiting for their owners to want to take them out to sea!"

"So, it's entirely the owners' choice isn't it?"

"Yes. Each boat looks highly equipped with every kind of technical device and there's even a fuel pump on the quayside. There seems to be nothing to stop them leaving the harbour."

"At Dunkirk, everyone who had the courage took whatever craft they had, however small, and went to the rescue. I did that through those who were willing to take a risk and put the lives of others before themselves.

Isn't it the same now? So many people around you stranded and frightened, the enemy behind them and they don't know the way off the beach. You know those I'm talking about. Some of them look fine above the waterline but below the surface of their lives there's so much pain. They have no purpose, no plan, just the perpetual darkness of existence that knows nothing of my love. If you'll take the risk and leave the quiet waters of the harbour, I'll chart the course for you on the open sea. I won't show you where we're going, you must trust me, just untie from the jetty wall and get underway. We'll go out on the high waters of faith, rejoicing in my power. I'll give you the courage to set your sails high, catching my heavenly breeze in every situation! I'll take away the fear that seeks to know where you are going. I am going with you and that's all you'll need to know!"

Joshua 1:9 Be strong and courageous...for the LORD your God will be with you wherever you go.

2 Corinthians 12:9 My grace is sufficient for you, for my power is made perfect in weakness.

Why are you clutching the thorns of guilt, when I'm holding out the flowers of forgiveness?

One early summer morning, sitting on our blue garden bench, I was absorbing the beauty around me: the fragrance of the tall white-scented lilies in their twin terracotta pots and the pleasure of throwing little pieces of my toast to the sparrows. Hopping and twittering in the twiggy branches of the wild mauve rhododendron bush, they were thoroughly enjoying their early morning get-together.

Suddenly, I saw in my mind an image of a beautiful, brightly coloured parakeet, sitting on one of the branches. It was so 'real' to my eyes that I wondered what it was doing there in my garden, as it certainly didn't belong to me. It looked so exotic and expensive – surely, someone had lost it and was offering a reward for its safe return. Into these thoughts, a gentle voice began speaking to my mind.

"No, this does belong to you! It represents the new abundant life I have given you by my Son's sacrifice on the cross. My love for you is far beyond your imagination, and yes, you were bought at a great price! I want you to keep this immense love I have for you in focus, throughout each day in both the difficult times and the times when all is going well.

Just as a ballet dancer finds a 'spot' on which to fix her eyes when she is doing a pirouette, both to steady her and to help her stay on the place where she's spinning, so too, you need to have your eyes fixed on me and keep my love for you in focus at all times.

The 'world' will spin you if it can, to make you lose your peace and your balance. There will be days when the wind blows up a storm of worry and frustration, causing you to be full of doubt and fear. Sometimes, these tricky little squalls are sent by the enemy to try and topple you out of your boat!

But I am in the midst of every storm in your life and I will use the wind and the waves to strengthen you in your faith and knowledge of me. If you keep your eyes on me and trust my word, you will see my 'rainbow' in every wave that hits your boat!

Don't keep criticising yourself every time you fail me in some way. I know your weaknesses and I am in the boat with you. Yes, acknowledge when you fail or fall short of doing your best, but don't hug these thorny failures to yourself. Just imagine that I am walking towards you with my arms full of red roses, and a smile in my eyes that says, 'With all my love and forever forgiven!'"

Romans 6:4 We were therefore buried with him through baptism into death in order that, just as Christ was raised from the dead through the glory of the Father, we too may live a new life.

Luke 12:7 Don't be afraid; you are worth more than many sparrows.

Am I allowed to make both elephants and butterflies?

It was after a talk by Jackie Pullinger at Holy Trinity Church, Brompton, in London, that I decided that following Jesus was too hard for me, I was bound to fail! I'd never rise to the heights of faith or obedience that I had read about in her book, *Chasing the Dragon**, or be able to work amongst the drug addicts within the Walled City in Hong Kong. I'd never have the courage to leave home, friends and family and be led by the Holy Spirit into a strange country and undertake a dangerous mission! I was feeling very sorry for myself, when a soft voice interrupted my despondent murmurings.

"Am I allowed to make both elephants and butterflies?"

"Yes of course," I replied, wondering what was coming next!

"Well, I have made you a 'butterfly' and you are not to criticise yourself for not being able to do the things an 'elephant' does! I have need of faithful, strong 'elephants' in my kingdom but I need 'butterflies' too! Be content with who you are and don't belittle yourself – be little and do the small things I ask you to do faithfully. Be freely available to me by not getting too busy and 'tied up' with fruitless activities.

The 'lifebelt' that I throw to a drowning man is the one that I find resting on its bracket, where it's meant to be. The one that is 'tied up' or 'gone missing' can never be of any use to me in my desire to reach out to those of my children who are lost and do not know me. I need you too to be willing, available, ready to hear and obey.

*Published by Hodder and Stoughton

The size of the work in hand is not yours to question or judge, you are not responsible for how or when I choose to do my work.

And I need my children's hands to be like mine – pierced with my purposes and surrendered to my love. Hands that bless, comfort, heal and impart peace. As you surrender your heart to me, your hands become mine."

Isaiah 43:1 Fear not, for I have redeemed you; I have summoned you by name; you are mine.

Hebrews 13:20–21 May the God of peace...equip you with everything good for doing his will, and may he work in us what is pleasing to him, through Jesus Christ, to whom be glory for ever and ever. Amen.

My love is like a warm conservatory:
a place where you can find rest
and be restored.

The Gatwick Express crawled past the backs of the identical brick houses, their long narrow gardens truncated by the elevated railway line. I gazed rather absent-mindedly into these bleak deserted gardens, searching for some sign of life. Occasionally there would be a splash of bright blue – a child's paddling pool now full of rain water, or some limp washing hanging out on a line. The veiled windows looked cold, the heavy, grey, January clouds adding to their gloom.

Then, I suddenly caught sight of an exquisite white conservatory, attached to the back of one of the houses! As it passed by I found myself smiling at the pleasure it gave me and I couldn't help thinking about it for the rest of the journey into Victoria Station. Whatever the cost had been, breaking out through that back wall and building that little extension must have changed the atmosphere of the whole house!

It reminded me of the beautiful, delicate tassels of white blossom, that in spring break through the crusty bark on our neighbours' cherry tree that leans over a wall into our garden.

"My dearest child, I know what lies hidden behind the walls of your homes, the difficulties and seemingly hopeless situations that drain the life out of you – the boredom of wearisome tasks and the discouragements that can so easily, slowly wither your hopes. Sometimes you feel that I am like a slightly critical stranger, indifferently passing by, an observer looking down on your life from a safe distance – uninvolved. But I am as close as you dare to imagine and have broken through the wall that separated us, making a special place for you to come into the warmth of my love to be restored.

Regardless of how you feel, resist the temptation to go back into the dark memories of your old life. For fear, pessimism and self-pity will surely clip your roots and stunt your growth. I have not called you to be a bonsai, but a mighty oak of righteousness!

As you praise and thank me, trusting that you really are accepted and beloved, the atmosphere around you will change, and protect the buds of this new life 'in me' from the 'frost' of grumbling, doubt and cynicism – for these will destroy both the blossom and fruit in your life. Let me be your conservatory, a place where we can sit and spend time together, where you can really 'be yourself' and know that I am for you and not against you."

Psalm 62:1 My soul finds rest in God alone; my salvation comes from him.

Song of Songs 2:10 Arise my darling, my beautiful one, and come with me. See! The winter is past; the rains are over and gone.

Like the 'magic' painting book you so enjoyed as a child, I too take up a brush full of water to reveal the colours I've hidden in your life.

The Café LaVille spans the Regents Park Canal in Little Venice; its curved black railed balcony hangs over the water, like the bows of a ship. On one side of the café, the canal gently rocks the brightly painted barges whilst, on the other, the traffic hurries up the Edgware Road, heading northwards out of London.

Sitting at a window table, warming my hands against my chocolate-speckled cappuccino, I could see down the whole length of the canal. The bright barges threaded their coloured, ribbon-reflections through the khaki waters. Three Canadian geese, searching for food, created beautiful sun-etched patterns on the water's surface. Except for the soft voices of two girls having a heart-to-heart at the table next to me, the only sounds were the dull background traffic noise and the voice of Engelbert Humperdinck singing, "Please release me let me go…". Clinking cups by the espresso machine and tinkling teaspoons at the next table added some percussion!

Outside, a barge unhurriedly coming down the centre of the canal finally slipped quietly under the edge of my blue tablecloth, leaving behind a softening trail of feathered ripples. This living picture spoke to me.

"Like the 'magic' painting book you so enjoyed as a child, I too take up a brush full of water to reveal the colours I've hidden in your life. I want to paint a picture of my love, in and through your life, and for all my children who will surrender themselves fully to my heart's desire for them.

I too want a close relationship with you – like those girls at the next table – so that we too may have heart-to-hearts! Out of this intimacy you will experience the joy-filled colourful life that I have promised you, and reveal who I really am to those you meet. Not a broken reflection, that changes with every light, but a wholly truthful replica of myself. My life lived through you, can only be fully realised by your saying "yes" to me. Allow the water-soft brushstrokes of my Spirit to etch my plans and purpose into your life, day by day. Let me write upon the waters of your spirit, leaving my messages of love for those who search with longing eyes for 'something better' for their lives.

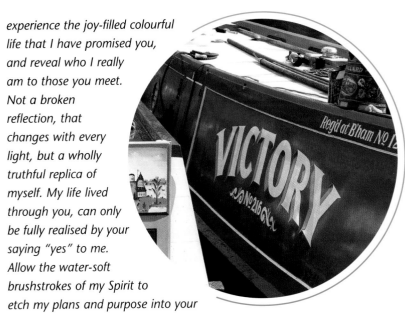

Do you want your life to make ripples? Then, cast off the rope that makes you feel so safe and secure and get moving! Don't be content merely to reflect yourself on the surface of these still shallow waters – leave your old moorings and take the risk of coming under the bridge with me!"

John 10:3   He calls his own sheep by name and leads them out.

2 Corinthians 5:17   Therefore, if anyone is in Christ, he is a new creation; the old has gone, the new has come!

My motto for you is to keep going! Keep hoping, keep praying, keep trusting, and keep coming back to my loving hand.

Shimmering summer arrived unexpectedly in early March and caught us all totally overdressed. Lyme Regis Bay, lying exposed under the cliffs, grew hotter and hotter. Ice-cream sellers developed 'out-of-season' aching wrists! Men discarded their shirts and two little children joyfully shed all their clothes and found that they had the beach almost entirely to themselves.

My cousin Marilyn and I, wrapped up in winter jackets and warm boots, sat chatting under the Cobb, enjoying being rather too warm. On the beach, the antics of a beautiful lively border collie kept us enchanted as she tried to rid the beach, and the airspace above it, of all the seagulls! Holding a short stick between her teeth, she leapt in and out of the sea, flinging sparkling salty spray into the air as she raced back and forth across the sands thoroughly enjoying herself. In spite of the stick, she barked continuously as she tried to frighten the birds off; it was very funny to watch her trying to round them up, as they paid little attention and tormented her by flying in circles above her head!

Finally, they left. Wagging her tail delightedly, the collie dropped the stick and, with her face wreathed in a doggy smile, she ran back to her master to receive a well-earned pat on the back!

"I have given you every spiritual blessing through my in-dwelling Holy Spirit. He knows my will, he knows the things I desire and makes them known to you. He longs to do my work through you and to give you the joy of being my co-worker!

Just as a shepherd and his dog need to work as a team, caring for the sheep, so you and I must work closely together to look after those I love. If you learn to listen to my voice and obey my commands, you will find that I will lead you into exactly the exciting kind of work that will give you and I the deepest pleasure and satisfaction. The scene you enjoyed watching on the beach clearly showed the collie's joy as she acted out her natural inbred desire to 'round up the sheep!' Even though the seagulls didn't respond in quite the way she expected, she didn't give up and persevered to the end.

You too must keep going, although at times you will be tempted by the 'seagulls circling in the air' – those fruitless distractions that will exhaust and frustrate you if you run after them. Keep going, that is my motto for you. Keep hoping, keep praying, keep seeking and keep coming back to my loving hand. Keep trusting, keep obeying and above all keep laughing!"

Ezekiel 36:26 I will give you a new heart and put a new spirit in you.

Hebrews 10:36 You need to persevere so that when you have done the will of God, you will receive what he has promised.

Look up from the hard stony path
and look for my messages in the sky!

The medieval village of Biot, perched high on a hilltop, is softly
contoured by olive and citrus trees. My friend Caroline and I spent a
lovely afternoon exploring this charming historic village, with its
souvenir shops and art galleries that brighten the streets with dabs of
stinging Provençale colour. The narrow cool passageways, with their
cobbled, uneven steps, led us past ancient wooden doors with huddled
pots of geraniums hiding within the overhanging lintels. Stone
buttresses and arches held walls apart as we entered into a maze of
little alleyways, only to come out of the shadows into a sunlit cobbled
terrace with an unexpected panoramic view. From here, over the
weathered tiled roofs, we could see the azure waters of the
Mediterranean, soft-rimming the horizon.

A lemon tree hung over a small, carved stone balcony, suspended
above where we were standing. I imagined Juliet leaning over it,
inviting Romeo to climb up and join her! But the only thing that scaled
the wall was a plume of jasmine, spiralling upwards, breaking into a
mist of tiny white flowers that filled the air with incense.

It was then, just as we turned to leave, that we saw a black heart-
shaped weathervane, fixed to the top of a perfect little square tiled
turret – silent as a blackbird waiting for evensong!

*"My love is not silent, it speaks to you at every turn, from every rooftop;
it scents the very air you breathe. It shadows you with protection in the
heat of the noonday sun; it surrounds you in the worst storms and stays
fixed to its pinnacle, whichever way the wind blows!*

*Look up from the hard stony path and look for my messages in the sky!
Open your eyes and turn aside, notice my fingerprints in everything that is*

beautiful and holy. Watch which way the wind is blowing, and be open to having your spirit filled with my presence. Search for the golden edge of my robe through your sometimes tear-filled eyes, for I have gilded every page of your life with my love. Lift my word up high in your heart daily; fix my truth above every other variable thought that passes through your mind. Trust me in everything that happens – however painful, and look beyond.

Beyond the darkness, there is light. Beyond the pain there is healing. Beyond your present despair, there is hope."

Deuteronomy 33:27 The eternal God is your refuge, and underneath are the everlasting arms.

John 8:12 [Jesus] said, "I am the light of the world. Whoever follows me will never walk in darkness, but will have the light of life."

Trust me, for I know the beginning of your journey – and the end.

The lighthouse and the chapel stand together looking out over the pine trees of Cap d'Antibes; whilst the white square tower of the lighthouse stretches upwards above the treetops, the ancient terracotta-tiled chapel below shelters within the aromatic umbrella pines. Both have magnificent views of the twin azure bays of Antibes/Juan les Pins and the ever-changing breathtaking backdrop of the French Alps. When the weather is fine, hooting bridal processions come up along the winding tarmac road for the bride to have her photographs taken in front of this majestic view.

There is a quieter, hidden way to the top – the Chemin de Calvaire. An isolated, rough and lonely pathway, it commemorates Jesus' walk

to Calvary carrying his cross. On a grey, drizzly day, I came up this steep, slippery path, meeting no one on the way. Except for the song of blackbirds and the poignant sound of a cock crowing once in the distance, it was utterly silent. At last, having breathlessly reached the top, I sat down to rest and look at the view. The mountains were invisible; there was not even the faint watermark of a horizon. Just a pale milky mist through which sailing boats emerged, drifting weightlessly in the air like paper mobiles.

"I know every stone of the way to the cross, my child, for it is here that I poured out my cleansing, life-empowering blood! I have left my footprints for you to follow on this rough pathway. Along this narrow way I give my bride her beauty treatments – and adorn her with her bridal jewels. For my plans and purposes for your life – to mould you to my likeness – can only be fulfilled when you learn to persevere and endure. At times you will be lonely and discouraged, longing to be joined by the 'happy procession of hooting horns' along the easier way. You'll want the world's praise and admiration, the comfort of warming yourself by its fires of approval – wanting to wrap yourself up in a sense of 'belonging'. But you will lose the sense of my loving presence, for I never walk along that wide, busy road.

Trust me, for I know the beginning of your journey – and the end. At times you will not see the horizon ahead of you, no landmarks on which to hang your hopes – no horizon by which to measure your progress. Remember that my word is the lamp for your feet – one day at a time – and a light that shines in the darkness steering you past the rocks of destruction; hold on to me for I am the only guide-rail along the way. At times, my best for you may seem to be totally out of line with what you think is being 'loving'. I still weep. I feel your pain long before it touches you; my hands are the crucible under which the fires of your refining burn. I love you, my child, trust me that all will be well when we finally reach the top."

Psalm 23:4 Even though I walk through the valley of the shadow of death, I will fear no evil, for you are with me; your rod and your staff, they comfort me.

John 19:16–17 So the soldiers took charge of Jesus. Carrying his own cross, he went out to the place of the Skull (which in Aramaic is called Golgotha).

Do not flap your own wings but rest on mine,
for I will carry you above the storm.

A sudden October gale had driven most people into the shelter of the old city of Antibes. As I walked along the ramparts to watch the storm, gusts of wind blew the salty spray into my face and hair; I had never seen such a violent sea before! Gigantic heaving waves bowed into green-marbled avalanches of water that rolled towards the high walled ramparts, battering them so powerfully that the spray leapt up over the top and rained onto the parked cars above. At the base of the walls' foundations, a large bright yellow buoy floundered in the swirling waves; ripped from its sea anchor, it was now ensnared by its broken chain amongst the rocks. Behind me, the weather-worn shutters on the old houses rattled furiously as they took the squall's full force head on, whilst the tall, whip-lashed palm trees were pruned mercilessly of their drooping, drought-scorched fronds.

Suddenly, some 50 white gulls rose up on taut-stretched wings into the air, whilst out at sea a courageous windsurfer flew by – a colourful butterfly perched on the crest of a wave! In the distance, on the other side of the bay, I could faintly see the small sheltered fishing harbour of La Salis. It was there, the previous afternoon, whilst sitting with my back against a sun-warmed wall watching the setting sun, that I had spotted a little blue and white fishing boat named 'Mon Roc' – 'My Rock'.

"So often your feelings rule your life my child and you get overwhelmed and dragged down again into despair and hopelessness. There will always be storms, how you react to them is what matters. Knowing my promises will help you to hold on tightly when troubles seek to overwhelm you or rip you from the anchor of my peace. Do not put your security in anyone or anything other than me, for no storm, however violent, will ever be able to separate you from the strong rock of my love.

I see the turbulence in your heart and mind when life gets difficult – people hurt or misunderstand you – an argument turns you 'inside out' with confusion and anxiety. Sudden sickness or financial problems change your life overnight – you feel 'lost and at sea' battered by troublesome thoughts. I know how fear makes you want to 'run into the city' to console yourself, when I want you to be strong and courageous – to get out your surfboard and stand on my word to carry you over the waves. What you may see as an insurmountable problem is not insurmountable for me! The pruning of the dead branches in your life is needed to produce more fruit for my kingdom – and it is always done in love – however uncomfortable it may feel at the time.

Ask my Holy Spirit to comfort you and lift you up on his wings – so that you may see and conquer each difficulty with my perspective whilst keeping your heart and mind at peace, sheltered in the quiet harbour of my unfailing love."

Psalm 18:2 The LORD is my rock, my fortress and my deliverer; my God is my rock, in whom I take refuge.

John 15:2 He cuts off every branch in me that bears no fruit, while every branch that does bear fruit he prunes so that it will be even more fruitful.

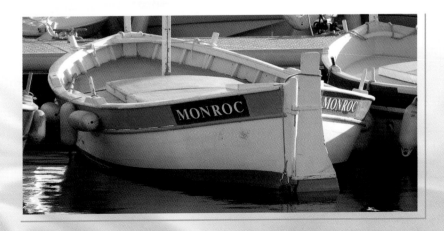

I kept all your tears in a bottle, and watched over you even though you did not know me.

After a delicious 'al fresco' lunch in the warm May sunshine, my friend Mona and I walked to the end of the cobbled street to visit the rare 15th century church in Biot. Having entered through its heavy wooden doors, we were amazed to find ourselves looking down into a deep dark vault, way beneath us, that glittered with numerous votive candles! Descending the steep stone staircase into the silence, the cool air wrapped us in wafts of burnt incense mingled with the fragrance of melting wax.

Because the lights were off and the famous masterpieces sadly obscured within the shadows, I looked up, and noticed for the first time, a beautiful circular stained glass window showing Mary Magdalene kneeling at Jesus' feet. Held up high above the ornate gilded altar, it hung like a 'crown' above the church, its jewel colours set ablaze by the sun.

The rays of light, streaming through the window, splashed its colours onto the stone floor beneath, where I stood in the dark. I thought back to the long years of depression I'd suffered: the black pits of despair, the senseless gripping fear, the loneliness – and the tiring hopeless search for a cure. The short-lived flickers of hope – a new medication or change of psychiatrist – had all come to nothing. I remembered the day when I hit 'rock-bottom' and cried out in desperation to God to help me, not realising that he had heard – that he had been waiting for me to come to touch his robe and be healed!

"I know all the dark days and nights of your life, the depths of your suffering when you longed for death and turned your face away from the light – when you thought you were alone and that nothing would ever change. I kept all your tears in a bottle, and watched over you even though you did not know me – when you didn't 'look up' or seek my face, but

walked by the flickering light of your own fires. I was at work in your life, even in those dark and difficult times, in the crushing hopeless despair, I held you close, even as a mother holds a sick child.

I have not led you out into the sunlight empty-handed, but with a jar of priceless ointment, a rare and precious perfume – for perfume is what I am seeking from the lives of all my children.

Perfume of love – perfume of praise – perfume of compassionate tears – perfume of quiet forbearance through difficulties – perfume of pain born for me – perfume of sacrificial love in your own garden of testing and trials. I create my perfume for heaven on earth – in the lives of my children. Thank me, that your life too has a perfume – a fragrant silent witness that draws people closer to me."

Psalm 118:5 In my anguish I cried to the LORD, and he answered me by setting me free.

Mark 5:27 When she heard about Jesus, she came up behind him in the crowd and touched his cloak, because she thought, 'If I just touch his clothes I will be healed.'

When the twigs look dry on the tree, they are not dead but waiting.

I love driving out of London early in the morning into the countryside of Kent to stay with my friend Fiona, who is a professional photographer. The rough track that leads up to her little white clapboard house is bordered on one side by deep bluebell woods and on the other by open farmland.

On this winter morning, I leant out of the bedroom window into the icy air; Fiona was already in the garden with her camera, catching the rising sun as it emerged from the fallow fields like a huge, red hot-air balloon. I hurried to join her, for all too soon it would bleach into a whiter light, diffusing the veils of mist that shrouded the distant woods. We watched together in the damp air as these vapours slowly melted away, revealing haphazard trails of stippled flint stones scattered upon the cold-stiffened earth. The stark shadow of the damson tree extended across the glistening wet lawn, stretching the empty little bird box, nailed to its trunk into a long dark silhouette. The beautiful landscape looked desolate and bare, waiting for new life. Some CD discs spun at random as they hung from the branches of an old apple tree – breaking into spectrum colours as they carelessly twirled in the early morning light.

"Up to now, everything that has happened in your life has just been a preparation. The ploughing up of hard ground, the winter frosts and freezing rains, all prepare the ground for new seed to be sown. In the same way as a ballet dancer softens her pointes, banging them again and again on a hard surface, preparing them for her feet, so too we have been breaking up the hard ground in your heart – removing stones, softening and shaping it for our use. We have done this through trials and suffering and the frustrations of on-going problems that have taught you to persevere. We know how painful it has been, that you have often felt that 'real life' was passing you by – that you were 'left out on a limb' – forgotten.

Be patient my child and wait, don't try to add your own colours into your life by seeking the spectacular or by stirring up your emotions 'out of season'. When the twigs look dry on the tree, they are not dead but waiting. Learn to wait in this wilderness with me, for I have not forgotten you or the plans I have for your life. My timing is different. It is like a bowl of golden oil into which I dip my fingers, letting the drops fall just at the right moment, in the right place, releasing the power of my Spirit, the 'sap of my life' into yours! I know when we shall walk out of this 'fallow time' for you will be leaning upon me alone, trusting me for the way ahead. But right now you are just where I want you to be. Wait for this anointing oil – for me to draw aside the veil and reveal myself. Be at peace. Trust my timing and be content for the moment to be my lady-in-waiting."

Jeremiah 29:11 "For I know the plans I have for you," declares the LORD, "plans to prosper you and not to harm you, plans to give you hope and a future."

John 15:4 No branch can bear fruit by itself; it must remain in the vine.

You'd like me to polish you into a beautiful stone, but I want to carve my name upon your life.

My favourite sculpture is Michelangelo's *Pieta* in St. Peter's, Rome. I have only seen it once, but I have never forgotten its beauty. I can remember the look of childlike purity on the Madonna's sad face, the heavy rippling folds of her head covering, her head bowed downwards to look upon her crucified son; her lowered lids veil her eyes, as she looks upon his polished lifeless limbs resting across her lap. The taut sash that cuts between her breasts emphasises the terrible hidden wound in her heart, into which Michelangelo has carved his own name.

Having dinner with friends recently, I was amazed to see a bust of this Madonna, only to discover that my friend Jules had sculpted it herself! The sublime look on Mary's face was breathtakingly lovely. Cast in

marble resin with added crystals, it sparkled softly with the sheen of real marble. I asked Jules if she'd been afraid of making mistakes, or if she'd ever thought of giving up? She replied that she hadn't, but had persevered until she had what she was looking for – the look of mingled sorrow and love on Mary's face. She added that it had given her a great sense of achievement and a deep pleasure, as her heart had been so enthralled in the subject she was replicating.

"I created you in my image in the beginning, and that perfection is always before my eyes in the face of my Son. Just as an unseen metal framework, an armature, was made to support the soft clay, so I too have placed my armature within you – the cross of my Beloved. It is upon his sacrifice of himself that you have received eternal life and it is through his brokenness that I am making you whole. I already see the likeness of my Son emerging from your life – like a butterfly from a cocoon – you are being gloriously transformed day by day!

Do not keep checking yourself in a mirror, my child, to see how you're progressing in this growing likeness to my son, nor worry too much about making mistakes! I am not hovering over your life with a red marking pen, waiting to strike out your efforts to please me with the words 'wrong' or 'you could do better if you tried harder'. I know what I am looking for in your face, I know how I am softening your heart with tears. You are not to fret or agonize in your struggles, or try to 'whip up' your feelings into a passion towards me, for you may often feel that your heart is full of yesterday's 'warm ash' and that the fire has gone out. Rest your heart and mind upon the finished work of my hands, and do not be anxious. Others may recognise 'the face of Jesus' in your life, long before you do!"

Isaiah 49:16 See, I have engraved you on the palms of my hands...

Ephesians 5:1 Be imitators of God, therefore, as dearly loved children and live a life of love, just as Christ loved us and gave himself up for us as a fragrant offering and sacrifice to God.

I alone hold the keys to your freedom and I long to set you free!

On a second floor balcony, above the Boulevard Maréchal Foch in Antibes, there lives a parrot in a large cage. Despite the constant traffic noise on the busy one-way street, I can always hear him singing as I pass by on my way to the market. Whenever I visit Antibes, even in the mild winters, he's on his balcony and I usually stop to whistle at him as I pass by. In the hot summer months, he has frequent siestas – silently dozing within his own soft warm feathers under the green canopy of trees.

In London, during a time of worship at church one Sunday evening, I had a vision of a budgerigar in a beautifully kept cage; there was everything that any bird could possibly want or need in that cage. The contented bird was happily pecking at a small mirror that dangled from a bar above its head, enjoying the sound of a tinkling bell each time it did so. I felt that maybe the bird represented 'me' in some way, and that I too needed to be set free. As I looked more closely, I saw that the door of the cage was, in fact, open and, as I began to wonder how to get out, a hand reached in and a voice said "Hop on the back of my hand and I'll take you out!" When I did so, the vision suddenly became very 'real' to me and I changed into an eagle flying at an exhilarating speed above the deep waters of a glassy blue fjord – it was absolutely thrilling! For a brief moment, I could actually 'feel' the icy air rippling through my feathers as I looked down into the white cumulous clouds that raced under my outstretched wings.

"I have come to set you free so that you can be fully alive – but sometimes like this little bird, who can only see its head and not its wings, you too miss my best when you look at yourself in 'small mirrors'. Dare to seek my face in deeper reflective waters and take the risk of sacrificing your 'comfortable cage' to truly follow me. Do not stifle the 'song of life' within you by becoming satisfied with food that doesn't nourish and a false security that robs you of my best.

Ask me to help you get out of any place where you feel trapped by fear or complacency; to help you give up that unhelpful habit you like so much! I do not ever condemn you, my child, but I long even more than you do for your freedom from every 'bar and door' that traps you. I understand your need to feel safe, but this kind of security leads only to a 'petrified life' instead of an exhilarating joyful one. Take the hand I hold out to you, for I am the way, the truth and the life and I'll never let go of your hand. I have so much more for you than you can possibly imagine – ask me to deliver you, for I alone hold the keys to your freedom!"

Isaiah 61:1 The Spirit of the Sovereign LORD is on me, because the LORD has anointed me to preach good news to the poor. He has sent me to bind up the broken-hearted, to proclaim freedom for the captives and release from darkness for the prisoners...

John 8:36 So if the Son sets you free, you will be free indeed.

I will always be your friend, it doesn't depend on your actions or behaviour!

The dark dawn storm had passed; now, as I walked in the sunshine up to the Botanical Gardens, towering light-suffused clouds sailed swiftly across the bright Monet-blue sky. Entering through the villa's creaking iron gates into the shady grove of umbrella pines, the warm resinous air mingled with the sweet scent of the wild freesias growing amongst the wet pine needles at their feet. I became completely captivated by this tropical paradise; I had never before seen such a profusion of wild loveliness and I was glad that I was alone in the garden.

I saw giant Chilean palm trees, their smooth trunks stretch-marked by the years, and the soaring white branches of the eucalyptus that swept the sky; wild flowers sparkled with confetti colours in the grass and the profusion of palms, flowering shrubs and towering trees was breathtaking! Beckoned on by the dappled light, I left the main pathways to explore the shadowy heart of the garden, where I spied what I first thought to be a little terracotta 'chapel', but it turned out to be an incinerator, its tall chimney blacked like a top hat! Behind it, almost hidden by a screen of whispering bamboo, I discovered the most beautiful stone well. The metal pulley on its heavy wooden crossbeam was completely hidden by a garland of snow-white clematis that hung over the dark glinting waters beneath. As I began retracing my steps back up to the villa, the nostalgic scent of a bonfire's ashen breath crossed my path, suddenly transporting me back to my childhood days with my father in our garden.

"In the beginning I planted a garden for my children, a beautiful garden where we walked and talked together and I still desire that intimacy with you now. I still want to walk and talk with you and I will always search for you when you hide yourself from me; I know full well how the Liar cuts across your path with his crafty whispers, trying to lead you away from me, back into the pit of darkness from which I rescued you.

He says to you: "Come looking good!"

But I say to you: "Come as you are! Bedraggled, broken, weak, sinful, resentful, bitter, angry, bewildered, sorrowful, doubting – just come to me!"

The Liar says: "You can't come like that! Brush yourself up, feel better about yourself, do a few good deeds to gain access, pay the price for the entry fee, after all, you can't just turn up with your muddy hands!"

But I say to you: "The further you've departed from me, the greater the longing and pain in my heart to have you close to me again."

The Liar wants to muddy the waters with guilt, to blur your vision and cloud your mind. But I am the ever-searching Father, the ever-forgiving Saviour and the ever-faithful Friend. And remember, even the muddiest puddle can reflect the light of the sun!"

Genesis 2:8 Now the Lord God had planted a garden in the east, in Eden; and there he put the man he had formed.

James 4:8 Come near to God and he will come near to you.

Return to me with all your heart!

Our journey to Cambridge for Rebecca Faith's baptism was annoyingly interrupted by an alarming noise under our car; now, dressed in our best for the lunch party, we stood on a dirt track some way off the motorway, whilst the legs of the RAC man stuck out from under the car. A motorbike parked just beyond us and the bikers, clad in black leathers, dismounted and sat in the sunshine on a grassy green mound a little way off. I glanced at them from time to time wondering why they didn't go into the nearby fast-food outlet for something to eat – but they just sat side by side, as if they were waiting for something. Quite unexpectedly, a soft voice clearly spoke into my thoughts: *"They're waiting for you to go and tell them that I love them!"*

I rather hoped I'd misheard and was glad when a moment later the mechanic slithered from under the car: "Nothing serious, I've fixed the problem," he said. "Would you like to take it for a quick test-run to see if the banging noise has stopped?" As I drove off, I hoped that the bikers might have left by my return – but they hadn't moved an inch! I finally got up the courage to go and tell them what I believed I had heard, expecting them to be off-hand or even rude to me, but to my amazement the woman said: "I've been away from God for a long time. I know I'm not meant to, but just this morning I opened my Bible at random and read a verse from the book of Joel where God says, "Return to me with all your heart,"* so just this morning I decided to return to Him. Thank you so much for coming over and telling us that He loves us."   *Joel 2:12

"A prayer of faith will always stop me in my tracks and turn me aside to meet with the one who touched me – however lightly. My mercy and compassion are always longing to meet even the most tentative act of faith. I find my children often in the most remote places, but there's no

place too remote for me to be able to feed them; not the remoteness of backsliding or indifference of heart nor of anything that has come between us. I know every minute detail of your life – your coming and going and yes, even your worry about what the possible damage to your car might cost you!

I had to stop you on your journey for I heard my daughter's voice calling out to me in the early morning. I couldn't wait to meet her and let her know that I had heard her simple prayer of faith, so I sent you to embrace her for me with my words of love and acceptance. You will never need very much to give away to others, but it needs to be 'fresh from my hand' like fragrant warm bread which I will give you just when you need it."

Psalm 139:2 You know when I sit and when I rise; you perceive my thoughts from afar. You discern my going out and my lying down; you are familiar with all my ways. Before a word is on my tongue you know it completely, O LORD.

John 6:33 For the bread of God is he who comes down from heaven and gives life to the world.

Don't let fear water down the 'new wine' I have given you to drink!

The fragile beauty of the early morning moon hung in the pale blue sky – its light as translucent as a bowl of watery milk. I'd taken a chair to the end of the garden to sit in the sunshine and, as I gazed up at the moon's beautiful veiled face, I realised that although I couldn't see its 'other half' it was not only still there, but that men may have actually walked upon it!

As it was such a glorious summer's day, I decided to drive to church through the leafy back streets of Notting Hill Gate, rather than taking the faster route via the motorway. Whilst driving I was still thinking about the ethereal quality of the moon when I was startled by the sound of rushing water and the flashing blue lights of a parked police car that blocked the entrance to a side road. A huge jet of water was gushing from a burst water main, spewing out stones and gravel as it flooded the pavement and rushed down the street, soaking everything in its path.

At the end of the service, during the final hymn when we sang the words, 'Set our feet on lofty places'*, a gentle voice began to speak to me about what I had seen.

"When you see only 'half the picture' in a painful and bewildering situation, you need to trust me and my Word for what you cannot see – knowing that I will never fail you or let you down. As you proclaim my promises 'out loud' to yourself, your faith will become as 'concrete under your feet' and my peace will flood your heart and mind.

The times ahead will be difficult and there will be a spiritual famine in the land if my children do not share the bread of my word with others. Satan would like you to 'pipe down', to flow in channels that are acceptable to him; he'd like to silence you, to stop you gushing out to others all that I've done in your life. He wants to intimidate you by making you fearful of being rejected or worried about looking stupid. But I want you to be bold and courageous, telling others about this river of new life that you now enjoy; I want you to break out even more than you already do; to break out of your old ways of thinking, so that I may 'splash' all my children with my healing contagious joy.

Don't let fear water down the 'new wine' I have given you to drink, for those who taste it will be thirsty for more. Above all, never ever 'lower the ceiling of your faith' so that you can touch it – believe in me and trust me for greater things than you can touch, feel or imagine for yourself!"

Isaiah 44:3 For I will pour water on the thirsty land, and streams on the dry ground; I will pour out my Spirit on your offspring, and my blessing on your descendants.

Hebrews 11:1 Now faith is being sure of what we hope for and certain of what we do not see.

*From the hymn *God of grace and God of glory*

Idols are put on a pedestal,
but I raised up my Son on a cross.

I can remember the day so clearly when my friend Charlotte and I
drove out of London to have lunch with Julie Sheldon in Kent. It was a
perfect June day, the sun was hot but there was a cool fresh breeze; the
soft green lanes were bright with yellow buttercups amidst the white
clouds of Queen Ann's Lace. We were able to sit outside in her garden
under an umbrella and, after a delicious lunch, we walked down to the
shady orchard at the bottom of her garden to see her Bantam hens.
Julie gave us each a fluffy little chick to hold in our hands – mine was a
very pale silvery grey. After we'd handed them back to her, she asked us
if we'd look for a chicken called Cleopatra who had 'gone missing';
Bob, the cockerel, was looking for her and was very distressed at not
being able to find her. So Charlotte and I happily looked for this lost
hen. We wandered through the long, cool grass under the apple trees
calling her name over and over again. As I was walking towards an old
barn, I was shocked to see a life-size crucifix leaning up against it; it was
Mimi's sculpture for her art exam – Julie had told me about her
daughter's sculpture, but I'd never seen it before. The brutal reality of
Jesus' nailed body was gruesome, his bloodied wounds so realistic that

I was moved to tears as I stood before it. His head was sunk deep within his collar bones and the gaping hole of his mouth seemed to still be gasping for air. As I looked more closely, I saw that his whole body was covered with pages from the Bible, which had been painted over with a coat of varnish.

We didn't find Cleopatra but Julie did; she was sitting in a large flower pot, up by the front door, laying an egg! I left 'death' behind me and walked towards new life, up to the house to congratulate Cleopatra on her latest arrival!

"My child, I do not want to get under your skin but into your heart! I did not redeem your life just by words but by my blood – by laying down my life for you on the cross so that you can now live a life of power through my in-dwelling Spirit. I want you to be a living sacrifice for me so that I can work through you and give this new life to others – so far you have only touched the surface of what I have planned for your life.

You weep over my wounds, but I weep over yours too; don't just believe the Scripture '...by his wounds we are healed' (Isaiah 53:5) without allowing me to come close enough to put my hand deep into your wound. My word is more than ink on paper – it is my life – so never use it as a 'veneer' to cover over your pain.

I do not want to be your priority, I want to be your all! When you desire me more than anything else in your life, you will become my 'healing vessel of oil' and 'reviving pitcher of wine'.

Acts 5:20 "Go, stand in the temple courts," he said, "and tell the people the full message of this new life."

2 Corinthians 5:15 and 17 And he died for all, that those who live should no longer live for themselves but for him who died for them and was raised again...Therefore, if anyone is in Christ, he is a new creation; the old has gone, the new has come!

When you feel that the waters have come over your head, raise up your periscope of faith!

Smartly attired in coats of glossy red and navy paint, *The Brigadier* was moored for us alongside the boathouse – it was love at first sight and I couldn't wait to get on board to begin my first canal-boat holiday.

At dawn, right beneath my window, the swans would come to feed with their young, gliding silently, ghostlike through the veils of the early morning mist. Having quickly dressed, I'd go for a long walk along the dew-soaked towpath taking my camera with me. In the reedy, shady shallows where the moorhens fed their cheeping chicks, the dragonflies flashed their sapphire fire within the golden beams of sunlight whilst the herons stood, statue-still, on a distant bank, their silver silhouettes mirrored in the still waters.

The meandering days were only punctuated with action when we arrived at a lock. Then, we'd take turns at winching up the paddles, allowing the rushing torrents either in or out, depending on the new canal level ahead. Sometimes, I'd stay on the boat as it sank lower and lower into the deep churning waters – exchanging a beautiful pastoral view of sunlit meadows for the darker, slimy walls of the lock cavity. Surprisingly, even in this unlikely place, bright green ferns sometimes grew out of the cracks in the walls. Only when the heavy wooden gates could be pushed open with ease did we move again – back out into the sunshine.

"You need to learn to seek me and find me in the dark places for so far you have only looked for me in the light; in the beauty of my creation and in the blessings I've given you. But I want you to go deeper now, below the surface into the hidden depths to find my presence even in the dark and difficult moments, those times of pain and suffering, situations when you feel that you are 'stuck' and that you will never come out into the warmth

and light again. It is when you are alone, in that dark place, that you must look up, to focus on my face and my face alone.

Out of your suffering I will bring something new and fresh, for this is when I do my deepest work in your heart. I have need of gloriously strong children and I use darkness and difficulty to burn up your pride; for your feelings do not lead you to purity, my child, but my fire does. Do not give up or give in to poisonous thoughts of despair and doubt – I am always working above on your behalf to bring about my plans for your life. Do not fear, I will never ever abandon you and, at just the right moment, I will bring you out into a new level of blessing, a deeper humility, with clearer eyes to see and a more compassionate heart with which to love."

Isaiah 43:2 When you pass through the waters, I will be with you; and when you pass through the rivers they will not sweep over you.

Hebrews 13:5 Never will I leave you; never will I forsake you.

The strings of heaven's music are within your heart!

It had been a gloriously warm spring day and the stone walls of the Saxon church were bathed in the dimming afterglow of dusk. The church, surrounded by fields and a few picturesque Cotswold cottages, was in such an exquisite setting that I stood for a while in the churchyard breathing in the cool evening air, sweetly scented by the newly mown grass. A pheasant squawked angrily from within the nearby darkening woods and a newly born lamb bleated like a crying child in a field on the other side of the narrow winding lane. The tilting gravestones, stippled and eroded by the years, were now beautifully embossed with little pools of gold and silver lichen and at their feet bright clumps of daffodils bowed their heads into the long wet wind-blown grass. And then a blackbird began to sing – the haunting beauty of its refrain echoed throughout the valley, ravishing the descending twilight with heavenly music.

During the service all the lights in the church were turned off and, having each received an unlit candle, we went outside to where a crackling bonfire blazed – its glowing sparks flying into the cold, star-lit sky. The vicar lit the tall waxen Easter candle from a flaming taper taken from the fire, then, leading us back into the church, one by one we walked up the darkened nave to light our own candles from his.

"From time to time you will see a glimpse of heaven, your heart will be strangely moved, your spirit lifted up in a sense of wonder and praise. These strings of heaven's music are within your heart, to be fully alive they need to be plucked often for in that way their divine refrain will reverberate through all the other strings of your life. Just as a harpist polishes and cleans the strings of a harp so that it stays in tune – so tune your mind and heart to things above and think about

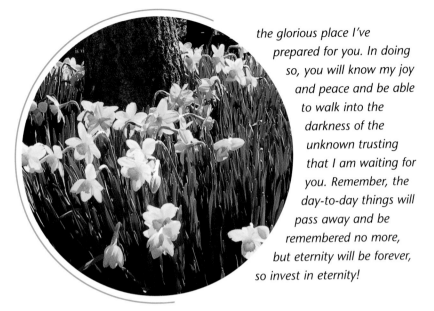

the glorious place I've prepared for you. In doing so, you will know my joy and peace and be able to walk into the darkness of the unknown trusting that I am waiting for you. Remember, the day-to-day things will pass away and be remembered no more, but eternity will be forever, so invest in eternity!

Remember my broken nailed feet and walk gently with others; offer a helping hand to them even as I offered up mine for you. Use every opportunity to encourage all you meet on the way, share your light freely without counting the cost. I've called you to be my light-bearer so don't put out another's fire with criticism or discouragement; many of my precious children will limp home with a smouldering flame and receive as joyful a welcome as those who run home with brighter fires of faith."

Isaiah 42:3 A bruised reed he will not break, and a smouldering wick he will not snuff out.

Colossians 3:1 Since, then, you have been raised with Christ, set your hearts on things above, where Christ is seated at the right hand of God. Set your minds on things above, not on earthly things. For you died, and your life is now hidden with Christ in God.

I've not asked you to be a busy bee but to be still and know that I am God.

It was late August – the leaves were warming to their autumn colours, the berries on the rowan trees already ablaze on the purple mountains. Sarah had lent us her secluded cottage in the Scottish Highlands where we idled away our days going on long walks or driving for miles along empty roads enjoying the breathtaking scenery. At night we fell asleep in a little alcove bed, listening to the flowing stream outside and to the scampering mouse in the rafters as the glowing embers of the log fire died down in the hearth.

On our last day, we hired a boat on Loch Shiel. The sky was clear and the water calm so we set off at full speed with a spare can of petrol stowed in the bows of our little outboard. When we were a mile or so from the place where we'd hired the boat, the weather suddenly changed; a stiff chill breeze sprang up and dark ominous clouds appeared and then the engine suddenly cut out. It was difficult to refuel the boat as it was bouncing up and down – the precious petrol splashing out of the funnel over my hands – but worse was to come – the engine wouldn't start again! So my husband, Michael, began to row back. I could see he was getting tired and we were making little progress against the wind and choppy waves and I began to feel frightened. Then, in the distance, we spotted a boat and seeing our frantic waving it came to our rescue; one of the two men had a full tool kit with him and by holding our rocking boat alongside his he was able to discover the cause of our problem – a dirty, worn spark plug.

"Just like this little boat that has been in service all summer long without being serviced, so you must look out for the signs of exhaustion that come from neglecting your intimate relationship with me. For service to me, and for me, must always spring out of your hidden life in me – in that way it will be my power working through you and not you doing things in your own strength.

Your friendship with me is far more precious than anything you will ever do for me; you need to fully realise how much I need your love. When you race ahead day after day without spending any time with me, getting busier and busier, going full steam ahead with your own plans – you are in great danger of burning out and ending up far from me, tossed about by stress and anxious about everything – you lose your peace and joy, and even draw others into your rocking boat of fear. Difficulties will suddenly erupt in your life but, by being constantly in touch with me, you'll be properly prepared for what lies ahead. If you do not nurture your faith by feeding on my word and asking for my help, you will have an empty' fuel tank' and be at the mercy of your feelings – but however foolish you may have been, I will always come to your rescue."

Psalm 46:10 Be still, and know that I am God...

Matthew 11:28-30 Come to me, all you who are weary and burdened, and I will give you rest. Take my yoke upon you and learn from me, for I am gentle and humble in heart, and you will find rest for your souls. For my yoke is easy and my burden is light.

When I stand outside in the cold, it is your love that keeps me warm and comforts me.

As I stepped into the warmly packed restaurant, I was met by the mouth-watering aroma of delicious food and the happy buzz and chatter of lunchtime customers; there wasn't a spare table in sight so I ordered the dish of the day from a busy waitress and told her I'd be sitting outside in the sunshine.

I'd just visited some famous glassworks in an old village and on impulse decided to treat myself to lunch and get a later bus back to where I was staying. It was so lovely to be warm after the recent cold, wet weather and, although I was hungry and looking forward to my meal, I wasn't worried that it took so long in coming, but after half an hour I finally realised that I'd been entirely forgotten. There was no one else sitting outside and I couldn't be seen from inside the restaurant as the blinds

had been pulled down to keep out the sunshine! I didn't feel like going back into the convivial atmosphere to re-order as it made me feel rather lonely, so I decided to take the first bus back to where I was staying. I stayed sitting at my table in the sunshine, keeping watch for the bus, in my mind I invited Jesus to sit in the empty chair opposite me and I asked him to tell me what was on his heart, what he especially wanted to say to me.

"My heart is for the lost, my heart is for those who do not know me and are shut outside from the warmth of my love. My child, you always sit at my table and feast in my presence and on my Word but many do not know me and know nothing of the food I long to give them. Just as you have been hidden from view and forgotten, just as you have been left hungry by the very people who should have brought you food, the same thing happens to my children! So be careful not to allow the blinds to be pulled down over the eyes of your heart by self-satisfaction or by seeking your own comfort before that of others. Seek to serve me first and bring these lost sheep to my table and I will look after all your needs; ask me to give you spiritual eyes to see those who are hungry and ears that hear the silent cry from an aching heart.

I cannot close my eyes or my ears as you can, my ears are raw from hearing the desperate cries of those whose lives are wretched. When I stand outside in the cold, knocking on the door of an empty heart trying to get some response, it is your love that keeps me warm and comforts me."

Matthew 9:36 When he saw the crowds, he had compassion on them, because they were harassed and helpless, like sheep without a shepherd.

John 21:15 Jesus said to Simon Peter, "Simon son of John, do you truly love me more than these?" "Yes Lord," he said, "you know that I love you." Jesus said, "Feed my lambs."

*It's only when you are out of your depth
that you walk on water and not on sand!*

At the end of the Rue Saint Esprit by the Cathedral in Antibes, there is a very interesting old door. Carved in relief on the outside is the figure of an artist opening the very same door – he's dressed in a smock and holds a paintbrush in his free hand, as though he's been interrupted in his work by a knock at the door. It reminded me of a time when the Holy Spirit challenged me about how deceptive appearances can sometimes be.

It was on a women's weekend away in Kent with my church that I realised that I often wore a 'mask', giving the outward appearance of being perfectly alright whilst on the inside I was feeling a mess. Diana, our women's pastor, had asked me to lead the early morning prayer meeting. Not wanting to let her down, I'd agreed, but I felt so empty inside that I wished she'd asked someone else. After years of suffering from depression, my Achilles heel is my mind and instead of 'taking my thoughts captive to Christ', a lot of the time they seem to take me captive instead! Crocodile Dundee explained it perfectly in the film of that name when he said that a 'croc' first drags you down beneath the water and wedges you under a stone to tenderise you for a while before coming back later to eat you! Well, that's how I felt – wedged under a stone with no sign of rescue and expected to be inspired and lead prayers that morning! On the Saturday morning at 6 am, as I was brushing my teeth, I muttered out loud: "I don't want to lead this prayer meeting and I wish I wasn't here at all!" I was very shocked when the following words entered my mind.

"That's the first honest thing you've said to me for a long time!"

"Sometimes, my child, you put our relationship on 'automatic' mode; you say the right things at the right time, sing the right songs and even raise your hands whilst doing so, but your heart is far from being open and real

with me. You open the door of your life just wide enough to receive the gifts and blessings, the friendships and love that you wanted, the talents and the work that I know you enjoy, but not quite wide enough for me to come in. You appear to walk 'arm in arm' with me, but your heart and your mind are elsewhere and I know it.

When you stop listening to my voice, you automatically tune into that old negative message that mangles your mind, that message that has never been fully wiped out. I see the safety chains on the inside of your door – chains that keep me at arm's length that stop you being real with me. If someone you loved asked you to go for a walk with him, how would you feel if he took you to a gym to walk on one of those treadmills? That is how I feel when you do not fully open your heart to me. I want you to be like a fragrant rose opening up to the warmth of the sun."

Psalm 73:25-26 Whom have I in heaven but you? And earth has nothing I desire besides you. My flesh and my heart may fail, but God is the strength of my heart and my portion for ever.

2 Corinthians 10:5 We demolish arguments and every pretension that sets itself up against the knowledge of God, and we take captive every thought to make it obedient to Christ.

Love is stronger than death.

The church at the top of the hill was built on the same site as the original wooden shelter that gave rest to early pilgrims on their way to Canterbury: hundreds of years of worship and prayer have steeped it in a breathless peace that flows into the surrounding ancient woodlands.

As you leave the car park at the foot of the hill, soft sandy paths muffle your footsteps, whilst fluting birdsong echoes high in the trees above. After a while, the narrow shaded path opens unexpectedly into a warm, open, sunlit pasture. We had prayed for my eldest sister to be healed of cancer, but now on this beautiful summer's day, we came to bury her ashes in a tranquil spot overlooking the paths where she had often loved to walk.

During the vicar's simple prayers, a small red aeroplane flew by, the drone of its engine intruding into the aching silence. I wondered if this might be a victory fly-past for a faithful woman who loved her Lord – a loving sign to say that Jo was alive – that it wasn't all over but that for her, life had just begun?

When the service was over, we began to drift away, down the hill towards the car park, when out of the blue the aeroplane returned. It hovered, momentarily, like a skylark, high in the sky, before beginning an amazing acrobatic display. Soaring and diving – it danced in the sky! Loop the loop – spinning on its tail, diving and free-falling – we could hardly believe our eyes!

Written on the stone above where her ashes lie are the words:
LOVE IS STRONGER THAN DEATH

"Your sister Jo is now rejoicing, she's begun a new life – she is thrilled and amazed by the glory around her. She is vibrantly alive and well – her eyes are bright with the Son. She is dancing – not in the sense of moving one

leg before another but shimmering in the lights that move around her, as heat moves above the road on a hot summer's day. She is completely absorbed by our love and light – she can no more turn her head away to look upon sadness than the sun can turn away from reflecting on the moon at night! She is now fixed upon joy and gladness. She has entered into such purity of holiness, that all else has fallen away, burnt up forever – ash blown away by the wind!

Rejoice with her, that will be the way to heal your own heart. All that is now hers will in a small but perfect measure be yours. This joy will cover over your wounds of loss and the wounds of all who love her."

John 3:16 For God so loved the world that he gave his one and only Son, that whoever believes in him shall not perish but have eternal life.

Revelation 21:4 He will wipe every tear from their eyes. There will be no more death or mourning or crying or pain, for the old order of things has passed away.

From the rising of the sun to the place where it sets,
the name of the LORD is to be praised.

Psalm 113:3